In the Spirit of
Christmas

In the *Spirit* of Christmas

by Dr. Criswell Freeman

Dorset Press

ISBN 0-7607-3736-3

*The quoted ideas expressed in this book (but not scripture verses) are not, in all cases, exact quotations, as some have
been edited for clarity and brevity. In all cases, the author has attempted to maintain the speaker's original intent. In
some cases, quoted material for this book was obtained from secondary sources, primarily print media. While every
effort was made to ensure the accuracy of these sources, the accuracy cannot be guaranteed. For additions, deletions,
corrections or clarifications in future editions of this text, please write WALNUT GROVE PRESS.*

All scripture quotations, unless otherwise indicated, are taken from the HOLY BIBLE, NEW INTER-
NATIONAL VERSION ©. NIV ©. Copyright © 1973, 1978, 1984, by International Bible Society. Used
by permission of Zondervan Publishing House. All rights reserved.

Scripture taken from *THE MESSAGE*. Copyright © 1993, 1994,1995,1996. Used by permission of NavPress
Publishing Group.

Scripture taken from the NEW AMERICAN STANDARD BIBLE®, Copyright © 1960, 1962, 1963,
1968, 1971, 1972, 1973, 1975, 1977, 1995 by The Lockman Foundation. Used by permission.

Scripture quotations marked (NLT) are taken from The Holy Bible, New Living Translation, Copyright
© 1996. Used by permission of Tyndale House Publishers, Incorporated, Wheaton, Illinois 60189. All rights
reserved.

Printed in the United States of America
Cover Design & Page Layout: *Bart Dawson*
Cover Photography: *David W. Middleton/SuperStock*

1 2 3 4 5 6 7 8 9 10 • 01 02 03 04 05 06 07 08 09 10

Acknowledgments: The author is indebted to his wife, Angela, and the rest of the Freeman family for
their support and love. The help of the wonderful staff at Walnut Grove Press is greatly appreciated.

For Mom and Dad
Thanks for the Memories

Table of Contents

$\mathcal{S}$ince you've taken the time to pick up a book that contains "Christmas" in its title, it's a safe bet that you're reading these words during the holidays. If so, Merry Christmas to you and yours. This collection of quotations and verse is intended to add a dash of inspiration and a pinch of perspective to the Season of Santa.

On the pages that follow, you will discover Christmastime wisdom from an assortment of clergymen, writers, composers, entertainers, and humorists. These notable men and women will encourage you to step back from the daily grind and experience the true spirit of Christmas.

If you take to heart the ideas herein, you will abide by the seven rules that I have, for many years, considered essential to the prudent enjoyment of the Christmas season:

Seven Rules for Capturing the
True Spirit of Christmas

1. Above all, remember that Christmas is a celebration of Christ's birth and act accordingly.
2. Amid the rush of the holiday season, slow down. Whatever it is that has your stomach tied up in knots is not worth it.
3. Sing at least one carol and buy at least one Christmas CD or cassette.
4. Make arrangements to be around children at Christmastime, and try to see the holidays through their eyes.
5. Don't overeat, over-drink, over-shop, overspend, or overstay your welcome.
6. Count your blessings, give thanks to your Maker, and demonstrate your gratitude by doing something nice for someone who needs help or encouragement.
7. And don't forget to write those thank-you notes!

Happy Holidays,
Criswell Freeman

In the Spirit of
Christmas

$\mathcal{C}$hristmas is a time for celebration and thanksgiving. On this day, we celebrate the birth of Christ, and we give thanks for His life and His message. This Holy day is the once-a-year birthday party of the Christian faith — it is first and forever, a religious holiday — a time for Christians everywhere to rejoice, to renew, to pray and to worship God.

The theologian Karl Barth noted, "Today, the Christmas message is delivered — the message of the light of the world which breaks through from above, always from above...." Each year that light breaks anew, and each year, if we open our hearts to the true spirit of Christmas, God's light will shine not only on us but also through us.

To understand the true spirit of the season, we must first understand the story of a humble birth that became the pivotal event in human history:

" $\mathcal{A}$nd all went to be taxed, every one in his own city. And Joseph also went up from Galilee, out of the city of Nazareth, into Judea, unto the city of David, which is called Bethlehem; (because he was of the house and lineage of David) to be taxed with Mary his espoused wife, being great with child.

And so it was, that while they were there, the days were accomplished that she should be delivered. And she brought forth her firstborn son, and wrapped him in swaddling clothes and laid him in a manger; because there was no room for them in the inn.

And there were in the same country shepherds abiding in the field, keeping watch over their flock by night. And, lo, the angel of the Lord came upon them, and the glory of the Lord shone round about them: and they were sore afraid.

And the angel said unto them, Fear not: for, behold, I bring you good tidings of great joy, which shall be to all people.

For unto you is born this day in the city of David a Saviour which is Christ the Lord.

And this shall be a sign unto you; Ye shall find the babe wrapped in swaddling clothes, lying in a manger. And suddenly there was with the angel a multitude of the heavenly host praising God and saying, Glory to God in the highest, and on earth peace, good will toward men.

And it came to pass, as the angels were gone away from them into heaven, the shepherds said one to another, Let us now go even unto Bethlehem, and see this thing which is come to pass, which the Lord hath made known unto us. And they came with haste, and found Mary, and Joseph, and the babe lying in a manger.

And when they had seen it, they made known the saying which was told concerning this child. And all they that heard it wondered at those things which were told them by the shepherds. But Mary kept all these things, and pondered them in her heart. And the shepherds returned, glorifying and praising God for all the things that they had heard and seen, as it was told unto them."

Taken from the Second Chapter of The Gospel of Saint Luke,
King James Version

$\mathcal{L}$ike the shepherds of old, we are called upon to glorify and praise God. When we do, we understand that the meaning of his son's life—and death—stands in stark contrast to the commercialism that too often obscures Christ's message. The following quotations remind us that the spirit of Christmas began in the unfathomable mind of God, that it was given birth in a manger, and that it lives today in the hearts of those who worship God and love His son.

*The light of the world is reborn in His glory
at the same season every year.
Let us bless each other and be joyful.*

Katherine Anne Porter

*L*et us pray that we shall be able to welcome Jesus
at Christmas — not in the cold manger of our heart,
but in a heart full of love and humanity.

Mother Teresa

*T*he old message: "For unto you is born this day in the
city of David a Saviour which is Christ the Lord"
is still the heart of Christmas.

Peter Marshall

A Christmas gift symbolizes the love that
Christians bear to one another,
in the name of the One who loved them all.

Donald Culross Peattie

The Son of God became man to enable men to
become sons of God.

C. S. Lewis

May the Christmas morning make us happy to be
Thy children and the Christmas evening bring us
to our beds with grateful thoughts, forgiving and
forgiven — for Jesus' sake.

Henry Van Dyke

It is good to be children sometimes, and never better
than at Christmas, when its mighty Founder
was a child himself.

Charles Dickens

This is Christmas: not the tinsel,
not the giving and receiving,
not even the carols, but the humble heart
that receives anew the wondrous gift,
the Christ.

Frank McKibben

Christ is the sun, and all the watches of our lives should
be set by the dial of his motion.

Thomas Brooks

Rejoice, that the immortal God is born, so that
mortal man may live in eternity.

Jan Huss

Christmas is about a baby, born in a stable,
who changed the world forever.

John Maxwell

*The miracle of Christmas
is not on 34th Street;
it's in Bethlehem.*

Rick Warren

Good news from heaven the angels bring,
Glad tidings to the earth they sing:
To us this day a child is given,
To crown us with the joy of heaven.

Martin Luther

*May this Christmas increase the
birth and presence of
God in your souls.*

Pope John Paul II

O holy Child of Bethlehem!
Descend to us, we pray;
Cast out our sin, and enter in,
Be born in us today.

Phillips Brooks

A Time for Giving

$\mathscr{C}$hristmas is a sharing time. During the holiday season, the whole world, or so it seems, becomes wrapped up in the business of wrapping up…gifts, gifts, and more gifts. We give big gifts, little gifts, expensive gifts and homemade gifts, here a gift, there a gift, everywhere gifts, gifts, gifts. Now, this gift-giving frenzy is good, up to a point. As long as we share our possessions rationally and with the spirit of joy in our hearts, and as long as we keep the reason for the season firmly planted in our consciousness, the practice of purchasing, packaging, and presenting presents is just fine. But we must beware of holiday excesses, especially considering the man for whom the holiday is named.

Christmas is the birthday celebration of a man who had precious little use for material possessions. Obviously, our emphasis during the holiday should be on spiritual rather than material gifts. Spiritual gifts (such as love, encouragement, support, and faith) endure, while material possessions, for the most part, are here today and all too quickly gone.

As The Big Day nears, your shopping list may seem like a plumped-up version of the Encyclopedia Britannica. If so, remain calm. Do your best, stay within your budget, and remember that the very best gifts are not necessarily the ones with the highest price tags. In fact, the very best gifts *don't have* price tags—they come from the heart.

*Material gifts are always secondary
to spiritual gifts.*

Rose Kennedy

To show great love for God and our neighbor,
we need not do great things. It is how much love
we put in the doing that makes our offering something
beautiful for God.

Mother Teresa

A happy spirit takes the grind out of giving.
The grease of gusto frees the gears of generosity.

Chuck Swindoll

I expect to pass through this life but once.
If, therefore, there be any good thing I can do
to any fellow being, let me do it now, and not defer or
neglect it, as I shall not pass this way again.

William Penn

It is the duty of every Christian to be
Christ to his neighbor.

Martin Luther

I always believed that the true spirit of Christmas
demands thought and effort on the giver's part,
not just lavish spending.

Inez Hogan

It is Christmas in the heart that puts Christmas in the air.

W. T. Ellis

Success has nothing to do with what you gain in life or
accomplish for yourself. It's what you do for others.

Danny Thomas

If you haven't any charity in your heart,
you have the worst kind of heart trouble.

Bob Hope

*P*roperty given away is the only kind that will
forever be yours.

Martial

*A*nd every gift, though it be small,
is in reality great if given with affection.

Pindar

*D*on't assume that spending twice as much will be
twice as satisfying.

Amy Dacyczyn

*W*hen I was a boy, we didn't have much, and
we didn't give much, but
what we did have seemed marvelous.

Bing Crosby

It's the spirit in which the gift is rich.

Edmund Vance Cook

It may sound like a platitude, and it may take
a long time to learn, but gifts of the heart are
the gifts that really matter.

Fred Rogers

...*So* let him give; not grudgingly, or of necessity:
for God loveth a cheerful giver.

II Corinthians 9:7 KJV

Love stretches your heart and makes you big inside.

Margaret Walker

...*See* that ye love one another with
a pure heart fervently....

I Peter 1:22 KJV

Every charitable act is a stepping stone toward heaven.

Henry Ward Beecher

Charity begins at home but should not end there.

Scottish Proverb

We don't give outrageously expensive gifts.
Christmas isn't a matter of showing off.
You should give of yourself, not just your money.

Andy Williams

Christmas is the day when any gift,
however small, should be gratefully received,
provided it is given with love.

Clare Boothe Luce

*There are all kinds of presents
one can get for Christmas.
The best is love.*

Helen Hayes

And now these three remain:
faith, hope, and love.
But the greatest of these is love.

1 Corinthians 13:13

Our children await Christmas presents like politicians getting election results.

Marceline Cox

Home for the
Holidays with
Family and Friends

$\mathcal{C}$hristmas is not a solitary holiday — it is a day best spent among familiar, smiling faces. When families and friends gather to celebrate Christ's birth, and when they do so with the genuine spirit of Christmas in their hearts, all seems right with the world.

Sometimes, distance and circumstance make homecoming a practical impossibility. A Christmas day spent far from family and friends serves as a poignant reminder that celebrating Santa's Big Day is a team effort: We celebrate best when we celebrate together.

Christmas day is a time to savor old memories and make new ones. It is a time to share a meal or two, a gift or two, a prayer or two, and a laugh or two. Christmas is a time to celebrate the ties that bind, and a time to tighten them. But, if for some reason, you can't be home for Christmas, don't fret. Just spend the day with your happiest memories of Christmases past, and while you're at it, pick up the phone, call an old friend, and talk to your heart's content.

Christmas is a together time.

Charles Schulz

Unless we make Christmas an occasion to share
our blessings, all the snow in Alaska
won't make it white.

Bing Crosby

The joy of brightening other lives, bearing each others'
burdens, and filling empty hearts is
the real magic of Christmas.

W. C. Jones

It is the personal thoughtfulness,
the warm human awareness, the reaching out of
the self to one's fellow man that makes giving worthy of
the Christmas spirit.

Isabel Currier

A family ought to be a lot more than
a collection of mutual needs.
It ought to be fun.

Art Linkletter

Christmas is being together — gathering together.
It is the time of the heart's inventory.
It is the time of going home in many ways.

William Saroyan

Surely Christmas is the very best time of the year
to be home with loved ones.

W. Herschel Ford

Christmas is the season of joy,
of holiday greetings exchanged,
of gift-giving, and of families united.

Norman Vincent Peale

A happy family is but an earlier heaven.

Sir John Bowring

Christmas is, of course, the time to be home —
in heart as well as body.

Garry Moore

This is the message of Christmas:
We are never alone.

Taylor Caldwell

Santa Claus is everywhere — but even the children might
get more out of Christmas if they knew more about
Him whose birthday it is.

William F. French

Let us open up our natures, throw wide the doors of
our hearts, and let in the sunshine
of goodwill and kindness.

O.S. Marden

Christmas is a day of meaning and traditions,
a special day spent in the warm circle of
family and friends.

Margaret Thatcher

A friend is a present you give yourself.

Robert Louis Stevenson

Friends are the sunshine of life.

John Hay

To celebrate the heart of Christmas is to
forget ourselves in the service of others.

Henry C. Link

To me, an old-fashioned Christmas means
old-fashioned values — like sharing Christmas Eve and
Christmas Day with your loved ones.

Robert Wagner

Compassion is the chief law of human existence.

Fyodor Dostoyevsky

Happiness is a perfume you can't pour on others without
getting a few drops on yourself.

Ralph Waldo Emerson

Christmas is a necessity.
There has to be at least one day of the year
to remind us that we're here for something else
besides ourselves.

Eric Sevareid

Christmas is a big love affair to remove the wrinkles of
the year with kindly remembrances.

John Wanamaker

God gave us memories that we might have roses in
December.

Sir James Barrie

When we recall Christmas past, we usually find that
the simplest things — not the great occasions —
give off the greatest glow of happiness.

Bob Hope

Something about an old-fashioned Christmas is
hard to forget.

Hugh Downs

The idea that Christmas is only for children is nonsense.
The longer we live, the more Christmas means.

Dorothy Walworth Crowell

Christmas is the keeping-place for memories of
our innocence.

Joan Mills

For children, Christmas is anticipation.
For adults, Christmas is memory.

Eric Sevareid

Christmas is the most evocative and nostalgic day
of the year.

Clare Boothe Luce

At Christmas all roads lead home.

Marjorie Holmes

Song and Verse

*W*hat would Christmas be without music? It's difficult to imagine. The old familiar songs remind us that Santa is on his way and that God is in His heaven. Each year, we sing the same carols, recite the same poems, and rejoice to the same hymns. We sing to our children and grandchildren the same happy tunes that our parents and grandparents sang to us. Music and verse become constant threads that link Christmas past to Christmas present.

Here, we celebrate a few of the most enduring lines of holiday verse. Happy holidays.

A Visit from St. Nicholas

'Twas the night before Christmas, when all through the house
Not a creature was stirring, not even a mouse;
The stockings were hung by the chimney with care,
In hopes that St. Nicholas soon would be there.
The children were nestled all snug in their beds,
While visions of sugar-plums danced through their heads;
And mamma in her kerchief, and I in my cap,
Had just settled down for a long winter's nap—
When out on the lawn there arose such a clatter,
I sprang from my bed to see what was the matter.
Away to the window I flew like a flash,
Tore open the shutters and threw open the sash.
The moon on the breast of the new-fallen snow
Gave the lustre of midday to objects below;
When what to my wondering eyes should appear,
But a miniature sleigh and eight tiny reindeer,
With a little old driver, so lively and quick,
I knew in a moment it must be St. Nick.
More rapid than eagles his coursers they came,
And he whistled and shouted, and called them by name:
"Now, Dasher! now, Dancer! now, Prancer! and Vixen!
On, Comet! on, Cupid! on, Donder and Blitzen!
To the top of the porch! to the top of the wall!
Now dash away! dash away! dash away all!"
As dry leaves that before the wild hurricane fly,
When they meet with an obstacle, mount to the sky,
So up to the house-top the coursers they flew,
With the sleighful full of toys,—and St. Nicholas too.

And then in a twinkling I heard on the roof
The prancing and pawing of each little hoof.
As I drew in my head, and was turning around,
Down the chimney St. Nicholas came with a bound.
He was dressed all in fur from his head to his foot,
And his clothes were all tarnished with ashes and soot;
A bundle of toys he had flung on his back,
And he looked like a pedlar just opening his pack.
His eyes, how they twinkled! his dimples, how merry!
His cheeks were like roses, his nose like a cherry!
His droll little mouth was drawn up like a bow,
And the beard on his chin was as white as the snow.
The stump of a pipe he held tight in his teeth,
And the smoke it encircled his head like a wreath.
He had a broad face and a little round belly
That shook, when he laughed, like a bowl full of jelly.
He was chubby and plump,—a right jolly old elf;
And I laughed, when I saw him, in spite of myself.
A wink of his eye, and a twist of his head
Soon gave me to know I had nothing to dread.
He spoke not a word, but went straight to his work,
And filled all the stockings; then turned with a jerk,
And laying his finger aside of his nose,
And giving a nod, up the chimney he rose.
He sprang to his sleigh, to his team gave a whistle,
And away they all flew like the down of a thistle,
But I heard him exclaim, ere he drove out of sight,
"Merry Christmas to all, and to all a good-night!"

Clement C. Moore, 1823

O Little Town of Bethlehem

O little town of Bethlehem,
How still we see thee lie,
Above thy deep and dreamless sleep,
The silent stars go by;

Yet in thy dark streets shineth
The everlasting Light,
The hopes and fears of all the years
Are met in thee tonight.

O holy Child of Bethlehem!
Descend to us we pray;
Cast out our sin and enter in,
Be born in us today.

We hear the Christmas angels
The great glad tidings tell;
O come to us, abide with us,
Our Lord Emmanuel!

Phillips Brooks, 1867

Silent Night

Silent Night! Holy Night! All is calm, all is bright.
Round yon virgin mother and child!
Holy infant so tender and mild,
Sleep in heavenly peace, sleep in heavenly peace.

Silent Night! Holy Night! Shepherds quake at the sight!
Glories stream from heaven afar,
Heavenly hosts sing Alleluia!
Christ the Savior is born! Christ that Savior is born!

Silent Night! Holy Night! Son of God, love's pure light;
Radiant beams from Thy holy face,
With the dawn of redeeming grace,
Jesus Lord, at Thy birth, Jesus Lord, at Thy birth.

Father Joseph Mohr, 1818

I heard the bells on Christmas Day,
Their old familiar carols play,
And wild and sweet
Their words repeat
Of peace on earth, good-will to men!

Henry Wadsworth Longfellow

Jingle Bells

Dashing thro' the snow in a one-horse open sleigh,
O'er the fields we go, laughing all the way;
Bells on bob-tail ring, making spirits bright;
What fun it is to ride and sing a sleighing song tonight.

Jingle bells! Jingle bells! Jingle all the way!
Oh! what fun it is to ride in a one-horse open sleigh.

A day or two ago I thought I'd take a ride,
And soon Miss Fanny Bright was seated by my side;
The horse was lean and lank, misfortune seemed his lot,
He got into a drifted bank, and we, we got upshot.

Jingle bells! Jingle bells! Jingle all the way!
Oh! what fun it is to ride in a one-horse open sleigh.

John Pierpoint, 1827

Adeste Fideles

O come all ye faithful, joyful and triumphant,
O come ye, O come ye to Bethlehem.
Come and behold him, born the King of angels.

O come let us adore him,
O come let us adore him,
O come let us adore him,
Christ the Lord.

Sing, choirs of angels, sing in exultation,
Sing all ye citizens of heaven above,
Glory to God, all glory in the highest,

O come let us adore him,
O come let us adore him,
O come let us adore him,
Christ the Lord.

Latin Carol, 18th Century

Away in a Manger

Away in a manger, no crib for a bed,
The little Lord Jesus lay down his sweet head.
The stars in the sky looked down where he lay,
The little Lord Jesus, asleep on the hay.

The cattle are lowing, the baby awakes,
But little Lord Jesus, no crying he makes.
I love Thee, Lord Jesus! Look down from the sky,
And stand by my cradle till morning is nigh.

Martin Luther

Matthew 1:18-25

This is how the birth of Jesus Christ came about: His mother Mary was pledged to be married to Joseph, but before they came together, she was found to be with child through the Holy Spirit. Because Joseph her husband was a righteous man and did not want to expose her to public disgrace, he had in mind to divorce her quietly.

But after he had considered this, an angel of the Lord appeared to him in a dream and said, "Joseph son of David, do not be afraid to take Mary home as your wife, because what is conceived in her is from the Holy Spirit. She will give birth to a son, and you are to give him the name Jesus, because he will save his people from their sins."

All this took place to fulfill what the Lord had said through the prophet: "The virgin will be with child and will give birth to a son, and they will call him Immanuel"—which means, "God with us."

When Joseph woke up, he did what the angel of the Lord had commanded him and took Mary home as his wife. But he had no union with her until she gave birth to a son. And he gave him the name Jesus.

A Season of Joy

$\mathcal{M}$ark Twain observed, "To get the full value of joy, you have to have someone to divide it with." His words are especially true at Christmas. The more Christmas cheer we share with others, the more we have left over for ourselves.

This holiday season, make Christmas a time of joyous celebration. Pull out the holiday music and take it to heart. Speak words of kindness and hope to every clerk, neighbor, friend, and coworker. Treat your family with a double dose of consideration, and lend a helping hand to those less fortunate than yourself. In short, turn your world into an extension of Santa's workshop and do as much of Santa's work as you can…this time of year, he needs all the help he can get.

Somehow not only for Christmas
But all the long year through,
The joy that you give to others
Is the joy that comes back to you.

John Greeleaf Whittier

*Christmas isn't just a day,
it's a frame of mind.*

Valentine Davis
From Miracle on 34th Street

All who would win joy must share it;
   happiness was born a twin.

Lord Byron

Seek to do good, and you will find that
   happiness will run after you.

James Freeman Clarke

Joy is not in things, it is in us.

Richard Wagner

Remember, if Christmas isn't found in your heart,
   you won't find it under the tree.

Charlotte Carpenter

This is the day which the Lord hath made;
we will rejoice and be glad in it.

Psalm 118:24 KJV

Christmas day is a day of joy and charity.
        May God make you very rich in both.

Phillips Brooks

Each day comes bearing its own gifts. Untie the ribbons.

Ruth Ann Schabacker

Though we travel the world over to find the beautiful,
        we must carry it with us or we find it not.

Ralph Waldo Emerson

The greatest sign of wisdom is continued cheerfulness.

Michel de Montaigne

Christmas waves a magic wand over the world, and behold,
everything is softer and more beautiful.

Norman Vincent Peale

The spirit of Christmas brightens even the darkest life.

Pamela Bujarski

There is no duty so much underrated as
the duty of being happy.

Robert Louis Stevenson

My advice to you is not to inquire why or whither,
but just enjoy your ice cream while it's on your plate.

Thornton Wilder

At Christmas, play and make good cheer,
  For Christmas comes but once a year.

Thomas Tusser

A Christmas family-party!
  We know of nothing in nature more delightful!

Charles Dickens

Christmas is coming. Unhappiness seems to be
  driven from our minds at this season,
  along with cynicism and negativism.

Norman Vincent Peale

Don't hurry. Don't worry.
  You're only here for a short visit.
  So don't forget to stop and smell the roses.

Walter Hagen

It seems to me the secret of a joyful Christmas —
especially for children — lies in preserving not only the
holiday but also the Holy Day.

Clare Boothe Luce

A merry heart doeth good like a medicine.

Proverbs 17:22 KJV

No man truly has joy unless he lives in love.

St. Thomas Aquinas

Merry Christmas to you!
May the glory that we celebrate in this
Christmas season fill your life forever and ever.

Norman Vincent Peale

My philosophy? Eat the icing!
Light those expensive candles!
Use those pretty little soaps! Wear, use, and enjoy!
There's no time more important than NOW!
Happy holidays.

Erma Bombeck

Heap on more wood! The wind is chill,
But let it whistle as it will,
We'll keep our Christmas merry still.

Sir Walter Scott

Joy is the serious business of heaven.

C. S. Lewis

Behold, I bring you good tidings of great joy,
which shall be to all people.

Luke 2:10 KJV

Be of good cheer;
I have overcome the world.

Jesus
John 16:33 KJV

A Season of Peace

In 1868, the clergyman Phillips Brooks composed a hymn that still warms our hearts at Christmastime. O *Little Town of Bethlehem* conveys the sense of peace that can — and should — be a part of every holiday season:

> O little town of Bethlehem,
> How still we see thee lie!
> Above thy deep and dreamless sleep,
> The silent stars go by.

The silent stars overhead serve as a true and constant reminder that God still rules His creation and His Son still offers peace on earth. That peace can begin with you — and should.

May we not "spend" Christmas or
"observe" Christmas,
but rather "keep" it.

Peter Marshall

Peace is the deepest thing a human personality can know,
it is almighty.

Oswald Chambers

When we learn to say a deep, passionate yes to
the things that really matter. . . then peace begins to
settle onto our lives like golden sunlight
sifting to a forest floor.

Thomas Kinkade

Christ brings lasting peace — peace with God,
peace among men and nations,
and peace within our hearts.

Billy Graham

Peace is not a season. It is a way of life.

Abbey Press

Let the peace of God rule in your hearts.

Colossians 3:15

Glory and peace.
>	Glory to God and peace to men of good will.
>		These are the immediate and
>		sublime effects of Christmas.

>					*Giovanni Battista Cardinal Montini*

Peace is always beautiful.

>					*Walt Whitman*

Peace on earth and mercy mild are still possible.
>		On Christmas Eve, all things are possible.

>					*Gregg Easterbrook*

Greatness occurs when your children love you,
>		when your critics respect you, and
>			when you have peace of mind.

>					*Quincy Jones*

I truly believe that if we keep telling the Christmas story,
singing the Christmas songs, and living the
Christmas spirit, we can bring joy and happiness and
peace to this world.

Norman Vincent Peale

*A*ngels come down, with Christmas in their hearts
Gentle, whimsical, laughing, heaven-sent,
And, for a day, fair Peace have given me.

Vachel Lindsay

*B*e perfect, be of good comfort, be of one mind,
live in peace; and the God of love and
peace shall be with you.

II Corinthians 13:11 KJV

$\mathscr{B}$e happy. It is one way of being wise.

Colette

… $\mathscr{T}$he cheerful heart has a continual feast.

Proverbs 15:15

$\mathscr{W}$hen I'm looking at a well-decorated Christmas tree,
no amount of adverse experience can convince me that
people are anything but good.

Andy Rooney

$\mathscr{T}$his will be the best Christmas we have ever had.
It has to be because it always is.

Ferrol Sams

*H*e who is filled with love is filled with God Himself.

St. Augustine

*E*ach year some new heart finally hears, finally sees,
finally knows love, and in heaven,
there is great rejoicing!
The Child is born anew, and one more knee is bowed!

Ann Weems

*T*he Spirit of Christmas is the Light of the world.

Dorothy Walworth Crowell

Peace I leave with you,
my peace I give unto you:
not as the world giveth, give I unto you.
Let not your heart be troubled,
neither let it be afraid.

Jesus
John 14:27 KJV

Calling Santa Claus

A little girl named Virginia O'Hanlon wanted to believe in Santa Claus, but her friends expressed doubts. So Virginia asked her father, "Is Santa Claus real?" When dad failed to give a straight answer, the young girl took it upon herself to write a letter to the editors of a New York newspaper.

Francis Church responded to Virginia's letter on September 21, 1897. Church's editorial has become *the* classic answer to the question, "Is Santa real?" Virginia's letter and Mr. Church's response appear on these pages, along with a few more observations about Jolly Old Saint Nick.

Today, as in Virginia's day, the ways of Santa are mysterious and, for some people, unbelievable. Somehow, Saint Nick makes million of toys in a cozy workshop with only a handful of helpers. Then, he comes down the chimney to deliver his goodies (even if no chimney exists). He loads countless toys into a modest airborne sleigh and completes all his rounds in a single night. Amazing. But even if Santa's methods are beyond explanation, his existence is never really in question for those who understand the real meaning of Christmas. As proof, we need look no further than our own hearts: when Santa Claus lives there, he lives.

Dear Editor, I am eight years old.
Some of my little friends say there is no Santa Claus.
Papa says, "If you see it in the *Sun* it's so."
Please tell me the truth.

Virginia O'Hanlon

Yes, Virginia, There is a Santa Claus

Virginia, your little friends are wrong. They have been affected by the skepticism of a skeptical age. They do not believe except they see. They think that nothing can be which is not comprehensible by their little minds. All minds, Virginia, whether they be men's or children's, are little. In this great universe of ours, man is a mere insect, an ant in his intellect as compared with the boundless world about him, as measured by the intelligence capable of grasping the whole truth and knowledge.

Yes, Virginia, there is a Santa Claus. He exists as certainly as love and generosity and devotion exist, and you know how they abound and give to your life its highest beauty and joy. Alas! how dreary would be the world if there were no Santa Claus! It would be as dreary as if there were no Virginias. There would be no childlike faith then, no poetry, no romance to make tolerable this existence. We should have no enjoyment, except in sense and sight. The eternal light with which childhood fills the world would be extinguished.

Not believe in Santa Claus! You might as well not believe in fairies! You might get your papa to hire men to watch in all the chimneys on Christmas Eve to catch Santa Claus, but even if they did not see Santa Claus coming down, what would that prove? Nobody sees Santa Claus. The most real things in the world are those that neither children nor men can see.

No Santa Claus! Thank God he lives, and he lives forever. A thousand years from now, Virginia, nay ten times ten thousand years from now, he will continue to make glad the hearts of children.

The New York Sun, 1897

There is something very real about Santa:
He personifies giving and
the spirit of the holiday.

Fred Rogers

*C*hristmas is sleeping with one eye shut while
the other eye watches for Santa Claus.

Charles Schulz

*T*here's nothing so beautiful as a child's dream of
Santa Claus.

Jay Frankston

*S*anta Claus is the fairytale that comes alive when
we are old enough to understand the magic of
our parents' love.

Ina Hughes

*N*ow the existence, the very spirit of Christmas is this:
that we first make believe a thing is so and lo!
it presently turns out to be so.

Stephen Butler Leacock

"Maybe Christmas," he thought,
"Doesn't come from a store.
Maybe Christmas…perhaps…
means a little bit more."

Dr. Seuss

Christmas Is...

Christmas is many things. It is, first and always, a religious celebration of the birth of Jesus Christ. As such, it is a day like no other, a day when Christians the world over rejoice in the advent of their savior.

Christmas is time to renew old friendships and to remember those who have passed on. It is a time for singing and laughing, a time for exchanging greetings and gifts. Christmas is a day of tinsel, wrapping paper, candles, greenery, home cooking, and lights...everywhere lights.

Christmas is a day for children, especially little ones, but it is also a day when even we grown-up kids can take time to recall those days when Santa was just about the most important man on planet earth, except, of course, for dad and granddad.

Christmas is the day when the whole world, or so it seems, slows down long enough to catch its breath and give thanks. God sits on His throne, the Christ child is born, the angels rejoice, and so should we.

Christmas, like God, is timeless and eternal.

Dale Evans

Christmas is a mood, a quality, a symbol.
It is never merely a fact.

Howard Thurman

Christmas is the day that holds all time together.

Alexander Smith

The whole meaning of Christmas can be
summed up in the miracle of Christ's birth.

Arthur Bryant

Christmas is sights, especially the sights of
Christmas reflected in the eyes of a child.

William Saroyan

Christmas is the season for kindling the fire of
hospitality in the hall, the genial flame of
charity in the heart.

Washington Irving

Christmas is doing a little something extra for someone.

Charles Schulz

The Christmas spirit — love — changes hearts and lives.

Pat Boone

My idea of Christmas,
whether old-fashioned or modern,
is very simple: loving others.
Come to think of it, why do we
have to wait for Christmas to do that?

Bob Hope

*Let us preach you,
Dear Jesus, without preaching ...
not by words but by our example ...
by the casting force, the sympathetic influence
of what we do, the evident fullness of
the love our hearts bear to you.
Amen.*

Mother Teresa

It is the duty of every Christian to be Christ to his neighbor.

Martin Luther

As you get older, you may think Christmas has changed.
It hasn't. It's you who has changed.

Harry Truman

Christmas went on and on as it always had and always will
forever and ever and ever.

Pearl Buck

Christmas, my child, is always.

Dale Evans

The Promise of
Christmas

On this day a child is born...

What begins on Christmas is fulfilled on Easter. The Christmas story is a story of hope; it is God's promise of salvation for His people..

Martin Luther writes,

> Good news from heaven the angels bring,
> Glad tidings to the earth they sing:
> To us this day a child is given,
> To crown us with the joy of heaven.

The promise of Christmas brings joy to the hearts of Christians everywhere. On this holy day, let us dwell on the blessings that God has bestowed upon us all, and let us give thanks.

The Christmas spirit that survives until Easter —
or after — is the essence of Christianity.

Isabel Currier

Our Lord has written the promise of the resurrection
not in words alone,
but in every leaf in springtime.

Martin Luther

The manger is a symbol of what can happen when
Jesus Christ resides in us.

Bill Hybels

If we surrender our hearts to God,
we may expect a wondrous enlargement.

A.W. Tozer

*I*f only we would look up, God is here. Christ is risen.
The Spirit has been poured out from on high.

A.W. Tozer

*T*he Christmas story gives its triumphant answer:
"Be not afraid."

Karl Barth

*T*hen let every heart keep Christmas within.
Christ's pity for sorrow, Christ's hatred for sin,
Christ's care for the weakest, Christ's courage for right,
Everywhere, everywhere, Christmas tonight!

Phillips Brooks

It is Christmas in the heart that puts Christmas in the air.

W. T. Ellis

At Christmas, Dear Lord, give us the faith of
innocent children. Let our hearts swell and let us live,
if only for a day, with the hope and joy
we knew as children.

Anonymous

If you have no joy in your religion,
there's a leak in your Christianity somewhere.

Billy Sunday

*L*ord, the celebration of the birth of Jesus is joyous.
During this time of thanksgiving,
keep me ever mindful of Christ's life
and His sacrifice.

Jim Gallery

*C*hristmas means the beginning of Christianity —
and a second chance for the world.

Peter Marshall

*T*he magic message of Christmas is that God gave us
so much more than we can possibly give back!

Norman Vincent Peale

At Christmas, surroundings do not matter because the spirit of Jesus is everywhere, knocking on the doors of our hearts.

Norman Vincent Peale

The one message of Christmas is the Christmas story.
If it is false, we are doomed. If it is true, as it must be,
it makes everything else in the world alright.

Harry Reasoner

Wise men and shepherds followed the shine of a star
which led them to a crib where they learned that
God is love. We still believe it, and on Christmas day,
we try to practice it.

Jessamyn West

The Nativity brings us within touching distance,
so to speak, of our spiritual birth in God through grace.

Pope John Paul II

The Son of God became man to enable men to
become sons of God.

C. S. Lewis

And Finally...

*W*e conclude with observations on The Best Day Of The Year and a stocking-full of holiday advice. Enjoy them, and have a very Merry Christmas.

The best way to avoid fatigue, panic, or depression is
to try to keep in mind that Christmas is intended as a
celebration, not a contest.

Sandra Boynton

Christmas needs a little less rushing about and
a little more quiet thinking.

Helen Valentine

Christmas is a good time to take stock of our blessings.

Pat Boone

Never worry about the size of your Christmas tree.
In the eyes of children, they are all 30 feet tall.

Larry Wilde

Don't buy anyone socks for Christmas.

Andy Rooney

Why not give a Bible for Christmas?

Good Housekeeping
December, 1959

Christmas is most truly Christmas when we celebrate it
by giving the light of love to those who need it most.

Ruth Carter Stapleton

As long as we know in our hearts
what Christmas *ought* to be, Christmas *is*.

Eric Sevareid

Christmas brings out the spirituality we sense within.

Leo Buscaglia

Every time we love, every time we give,
it's Christmas.

Dale Evans

We should try to hold on to the Christmas spirit, not just one day a year, but all 365.

Mary Martin

If you can keep Christmas for a day, why not always?

Henry van Dyke

They err who think Santa Claus comes down through the chimney; he really enters through the heart.

Mrs. Paul M. Ell

Gifts of time and love are surely
the basic ingredients of a truly
merry Christmas.

Peg Bracken

As fits the holy Christmas birth,
Be this, good friends, our carol still —
Be peace on earth, be peace on earth,
To men of gentle will.

William Makepeace Thackeray

Peace is our final good.

St. Augustine

Peace, like every other rare and precious thing,
doesn't come to you. You have to go and get it.

Faith Forsyte

On this Christmas, may we, the people of every race,
nation, and religion, learn to love one another and
to forgive and be forgiven.
Then, the peace of Christ will prevail.

Coretta Scott King

What sweeter music can we bring
Than a carol for to sing
The birth of this our heavenly king.

Robert Herrick

We must banish doubt and fear, and we must still believe
in the Golden Rule for all mankind.
Then, it can be a happy Christmas.

Franklin D. Roosevelt

And so, at this Christmastime, I greet you.
Not quite as the world sends greetings, but with the
prayer that for you, now and forever,
the day breaks and shadows flee away.

Fra Giovanni

We must all continue, especially at this time of year,
to try and fulfill this grand dream:
Peace on earth.

Elizabeth Taylor

Christmas makes the rest of the year worthwhile.

Charles Shulz

The joy of the Lord is your strength.

Nehemiah 8:10

Joy is the flag you fly when the Prince of Peace is
in residence within your heart.

Wilfred Peterson

Don't deprive yourself of the joy of giving.

Michael Greenberg

*Give yourself at Christmas;
there really is no more wonderful gift.*

Dorothy Wilson

The hunt for the Christmas tree: what a joyous day!

Mary Lindsay Hoffman

One of the nicest things about a Christmas tree is
    that it looks good no matter how you decorate it.

Phillip Snyder

The perfect Christmas tree?
        All Christmas trees are perfect!.

Charles N. Barnard

*Christmas is a box of tree ornaments
that have become part of the family.*

Charles Schulz

This is the essence of the Christmas story:
a spirit of giving; giving not from
a sense of duty, not as a return for receiving,
but from an awareness that in a world
where so much is given to man, man, too,
should himself give gifts.

Anne Bryan McCall

The most precious gift you can give your children
at Christmas is one that will stand by them for all times,
in all places and all conditions:
the gift of positive thinking.

Norman Vincent Peale

Here's my advice:
Make a big thing of Christmas,
even if you're tired.

Harry Reasoner

Christmas, my child, is love in action.

Dale Evans

"*God bless us every one,*"
said Tiny Tim.

Charles Dickens

Merry Christmas

About the Author

Criswell Freeman is a Doctor of Clinical Psychology living in Nashville, Tennessee. In addition to this text, Dr. Freeman is also the author of many other books, including his bestselling self-help book, *When Life Throws You a Curveball, Hit It!*